Adelma Grenier Simmons

Herbs Are Forever

Caprilands' Guide to Growing and Preserving

Photographed by George Gregory Wieser

Oct. 10, 1992
To Gillan Bradley
from your Mother
with Love.

D0950080

MALLARD PRESS

MALLARD PRESS
An Imprint of BDD Promotional Book Company, Inc.
666 Fifth Avenue
New York, NY 10103

This book is meant to be educational in nature and is in no way meant to be used for self-treatment or self-diagnosis. Keep in mind that excess quantities of some herbs can be dangerous. The editors have attempted to include, wherever appropriate, cautions and guidelines for using the herbs and herbal recipes in the book. Yet, we realize that it is impossible for us to antic-ipate every conceivable use of herbs and every possible prob-lem any use could cause. Moreover, we cannot know just what kinds of physical reactions or allergies some of you might have to substances discussed in this book.

For this reason, Mallard Press cannot assume responsibility for the effects of using the herbs or other information in this book. And we urge that all potentially serious health problems be managed by a physician.

Copyright © 1992 by Adelma Grenier Simmons
Photographs copyright © 1992 by
George Gregory Wieser

Produced by Wieser & Wieser, Inc.
118 East 25th Street,
New York, NY 10010

Editorial Development by Beverly Pennacchini
Design, Typography and Production by Tony Meisel
Photographic Styling by Laurie Pepin

Mallard Press and its accompanying design and logo are
trademarks of the BDD Promotional Book Company, Inc.
First published in the United States of America
in 1992 by The Mallard Press.

ISBN 0-7924-5615-7

Contents

Herbs Are Forever

Happy is the herb gardener through all the seasons and the years. That person enjoys a life enriched with rare fragrances at dawn, dusk and in the heat of noon. Each season bears an individual and special meaning, and each presents the gardener with gifts, uniquely its own.

From the bleakness of early spring to the richness of October, and far into winter, the herb garden continues. Long after the first frosts have destroyed summer's floral borders, the wreaths, vinegars, teas and jellies made from the preserved bounty of the garden warm the melancholy cold of the season and hint at the coming of spring.

Without moving from a sunny windowsill, or a chair by the fire, you may plant an herb garden as small or large as your imagination reaches. Plan and plant your gardens, sow your seeds, and enjoy your harvests. Make seasonings, vinegars, mustards, jellies, decorations, sweet jars and pomanders to suit your own needs, and whims, according to the size and shape of your herbal imaginings.

Drying Herbs

Drying home-grown herbs is one of the great pleasures of herb gardening. It is rewarding to use your own fresh seasonings to flavor your stews and casseroles throughout the year. Drying processes are simple, and the work need not be done all at once, for plants mature at different times.

Around St. Michael's Day, September 29, the busiest time of the drying season, Caprilands is decked in harvested herbs. Basil, savory, and mint hang from the kitchen rafters. Sage for holiday seasonings and flowers to add color to winter arrangements provide fragrant and beautiful table arrangements while drying for later use.

Culinary herbs are bent into wreaths and hung in the kitchen, to be picked as needed throughout the winter. The air is filled with good harvest smells and with the opening of the kitchen door the heady incense of heated spice and baking herb bread is wafted through the house.

Rosemary

Tender perennial, 3 to 6 feet. Needle-like leaves vary in color from gray-green to dark green. The blossoms may be white-rose or pale lavender. Root cuttings in sand or vermiculite using 3to 4-inch pieces of new wood or healthy tips. Prefers full sun to partial shade with evenly moist, well-drained and alkaline soil.

Cut plants before noon, after the dew has dried but before the sun has leached the essential oils. Wash quickly in cool water. Spread leaves thinly on a tray of fine wire mesh and place in a slow oven (heat should not exceed 150 degrees). Drying should be completed within a matter of minutes. Dried rosemary needles are sharp if left whole; I run these through a coffee grinder and they emerge at just about the right length for coating a chicken, seasoning a gravy, or spooning out for tea. Store out of sunlight in an airtight container. Herbs to dry in trays include chervil, lovage, myrrh, lemon verbena, parsley, and thyme.

Caraway

Hardy biennial, 1 to 3 feet. Furrowed stems with finely cut leaves. Umbels of white flowers. Sow seeds in September for an early spring crop of leaves and seeds the following summer. Prefers full sun and average, well-drained garden soil.

Harvest the whole plant immediately after heads are mature. Place it, seed head down, in a paper bag so as to catch all the seeds. Hang up until dry and the seeds will drop out readily. Be vigilant and harvest promptly or seeds will fall to the ground and be lost. Herb seeds to dry include those of coriander, cumin, dill and fennel.

Oregano

Hardy perennial, 2 feet. Leaves dull, gray-green, oval, flowers pink, white or purple. Propagate by division of established plants in the spring, by rooting cuttings, or by sowing seeds. Prefers full sun and average garden soil, on the dry side and always well-drained.

Harvest herbs at noon and wash in cool water. Tie in loose bunches which are decorative hung from ceiling rafters or strung on a pole across the front of a fireplace. Be careful, however, not to let them collect dust. Dry in the shade, but not in a damp place, as this will slow drying time. Remove leaves from stems and store in airtight jars.

Other seasonings that dry well in bunches include sage, savory, mint, marjoram, basil, lemon balm, and horehound.

Christmas Confetti Casserole

3 medium onions, sliced
1 cup celery, chopped
1/4 pound butter
1 teaspoon dried basil
1/2 teaspoon dried marjoram
1 cup fresh parsley, chopped
1/2 teaspoon black pepper, freshly ground
1/2 cup pineapple chunks
4 pimentos, chopped
6 cups rice, cooked
1/2 cup almonds, blanched and slivered

Prepare the sauce by cooking the onions and celery in the butter until soft. Add the basil, marjoram, half the parsley, and the pepper. Stir in the pineapple and pimentos. Pour the sauce over the rice, and fluff with a fork until the rice is well coated. Correct the seasoning as needed. Put in ovenproof casserole. Spread the almonds over the rice, and sprinkle on the rest of the parsley. Hint: For an all-in-one meal, add 2 cups chopped, cooked chicken or tuna fish to the sauce. Add chives from the window box; dried parsley also may be used. Bake in 350 oven for 30-45 minutes until hot and bubbling. Serves 8-12

Freezing Herbs

Freezing is a simple process and most effective for sorrel, basil, parsley, dill chives, mint and chervil. Wash these lightly, then place on paper towels to drain and dry thoroughly. Do not blanche these leafy herbs as it has a tendency to make them soft and it is not necessary. Freeze separate leaves or whole branches in plastic bags as you do with parsley. Do not overcrowd the herbs, and be sure you lay them flat. Keep them frozen until it is time to use them. It is best, when freezing, to determine how much is usually used at a time in order not to waste the precious leaves. Herbs that are commonly used together may be frozen in the same packages. Be sure that you label each kind and pack them together. Unless you are very accustomed to their appearances, they can be confusing.

Mint

There are many, divergent types of mint, ranging from pineapple, to orange, from pennyroyal to peppermint. Their various uses range from spicing May punch bowls to warding off insects. Mint is a hardy perennial with divergent leaves but normally leaves are dark green, sometimes velvet sometimes smooth, and often splotched white. Stems often turn purple in the fall. Blossoms range from gray-white to pale purple.

Mint will grow almost anywhere. They thrive in humusy soil in shade, but also in sun and few pests ever bother them. Propagate from cuttings in spring. The only problem with mints is that they spread too rapidly, over running other plants and growing into a mass instead of staying in neat separate clumps. To avoid this, it is suggested you plant each clump of mint in a metal barrel, with top and bottom removed and sunk 18 inches into the ground.

Mint is cut in summer to make jellies, vinegars, and an essence for lamb sauce. Leaves are candied and also dried for teas. One method we have found very attractive for punch is to freeze small sprigs of mint in a cube of ice. The cube, when removed from the freezer will melt, leaving the herb ready to use, or if left frozen makes an attractive and useful garnish for the punch bowl. You can also freeze borage flowers, violas and tiny marigolds, which are more decorative then flavorful with the ice cube method.

Orange Mint Punch

1 cup orange mint leaves
2 tablespoons honey
2 cups water
6 tea bags decaffeinated tea
12 cups boiling water
12 ounces orange juice

Mix mint, honey and two cups water in a large saucepan. Simmer over low heat for 10 minutes. Remove from heat. Add tea bags and boiling water to mint mixture. Allow to cool for about 1/2 hour. Remove tea bags, then add orange juice and mix well. Refrigerate until cold. To serve, pour orange tea over a cube of ice with a mint sprig frozen inside.

Sorrel

French sorrel is a native of southern France, Switzerland, and Germany. It is a hardy perennial, 2 feet in height. It resembles the related and common dock of the fields. Leaves are succulent, long and shield-shaped, a light green color, sometimes veined with red. Flowers are like dock but smaller, softer in appearance, and a warm red-brown color.

Prefers sun to partial shade in rich, well-drained soil. Buy a plant, then allow it to multiply. It is difficult to obtain seeds of the true variety. Broad leaf garden sorrel is a good substitute.

Cut early in the spring and freeze leaves for later use in the year. At Caprilands, we freeze sorrel in large quantities for sorrel soup and bouillon. In our experience sorrel loses a little of its tangy sharp taste during processing. When substituting frozen sorrel for fresh in a recipe, it's best to use somewhat more than the fresh herb called for. Freeze sorrel leaves in plastic freezer bags.

Parsley

Curly parsley is a hardy biennial usually cultivated as an annual. It has bright green, tightly curled leaves. Italian parsley, also a hardy biennial cultivated as an annual, has large, fern-like leaves.

Parsley prefers full sun or partial shade in humusy, moist soil. To grow from seeds, broadcast or plant in shallow drills in well-prepared soil. Sow in midsummer for autumn cutting and to have small plants to bring inside for winter window boxes; for an early summer crop, sow seeds in earliest spring.

Parsley can be dried or frozen. Freeze either by the ice cube method in sprigs for garnish, or, as one of our assistants does, whose experience with herbs is of long standing, freeze in a ball and then shave off the desired amount as needed.

Herbal Teas

The tea ceremony is a ritual not only for the Oriental and the English, but for herb gardeners and their friends the world over. The connoisseur of tea finds the garden, the woods and the fields filled with leaves and blossoms to lend their essences to fine brews.

For me, herb tea will always be associated with winter sunsets. Others have a cup ready on the kitchen table to sip during a busy day, or remember special times when, in a shadowy old house on a wet spring day, with the garden practically swimming, they have spent a pleasant hour drinking tea from an old brown Staffordshire.

Camomile

Camomile is a creeping perennial, about 1 inch high, except to 12 inches while in bloom. Foliage is fine and fern-like. The flowers are white daisies with yellow centers.

Camomile prefers sun to partial shade in moist, well-drained soil. Sow seeds in spring or fall, or purchase plants. Once established, camomile will self-sow.

The mature flowers of two plants, Chrysanthemum parthenium and Antheis nobilis, are harvested for tea. The petals disappear when dry and only the yellow seed heads remain. They yield a slightly bitter brew that is refreshing for headaches and nausea, good for the nerves, and soporific. This is a household medicine and one of the most popular drinks in Europe. Allow a heaping teaspoonful of the seed heads to a cup of water; brew in a teapot. Strain before serving.

Calendula

Calendula officinalis is a small-flowered, Mediterranean plant from which the large-flowered garden hybrids came. The flowers, of varying shades of yellow and orange, open and at dawn and close in the evening.

Calendulas are annuals and may be sown from seed in the fall. They bloom more quickly in rich soil They will survive light frost. When harvesting, pick them at noon when they are fully open.

I use this herb, with mints, in making tea. In the past it was used as an aid to complexion beauty, and is said to be healing to the heart and good for the spirit. Both the large and small-flowered varieties make a good tea and add bright color to herbal mixtures. I dry calendula blossoms all through the summer and even into late fall, for they often bloom after frost has killed every other flower. I store the dried petals in airtight jars and have them ready to use in tea mixtures at the rate of 1/2 teaspoon per cup.

Lemon Balm

A hardy perennial, 1 to 2 feet, with branches growing on a square stem. Leaves broadly heart-shaped, toothed, 1 to 3 inches long. Flowers inconspicuous, white or yellowish, off and on from June to October.

Lemon balm grows freely in any soil, but best in a well-drained location. Needs sun half a day, but will grow in shade. When plants are in a flower border, they need to be cut back to keep the foliage a good color as it has a tendency to turn yellow after flowering. Propagate by transplanting self-sown seedlings, or by sowing seeds (germination is slow).

I prefer to use lemon balm green for tea, but dry will also work. Pour 1 pint of boiling water over 1 ounce of the leaves. Let this steep for 10 minutes. Strain. Sweeten with honey. Lemon balm tea is recommended for feverish colds.

Mint Tea

Mint is the herb most associated with teas. It is the strongest of the flavors and in its own right without other herbs, makes a good drink for those who wish to replace China tea or coffee as a beverage. Apple mint makes an especially good tea. We cut it about three times in the season and store the leaves in air-tight cans and in the winter, use it in concert with other herbs, or on its own. Pour 1 pint of boiling water over 1 ounce of leaves. Let this steep for 10 minutes and strain.

Herbal Oils and Vinegars

Throughout the summer our visitors at Caprilands are intrigued by the presence of gallons of what appears to be water, placed in the garden, among the plantings of basil, tarragon, mints, dill and chives. This is distilled vinegar waiting for the herbs to be placed in it as they mature.

As plants are harvested, we place leaves in a bottle of the vinegar and allow it to steep in the sun. After a week, the vinegar is ready to be stored in a cool cellar where it sits until it is time to place it in smaller, individual bottles. It then comes to the kitchen where it is strained to remove old leaves and any sediment. We pour it through a funnel into smaller containers that may come directly to the table. We place a piece of fresh herb in each bottle to add a decorative and extra added freshness to the final bottling.

Preserving herbs in cooking oils provides cooks with excellent assistance in food preparation. A bland, flavorless oil is a good medium for herbal flavorings. When herbs are fresh, it takes about two weeks for them to permeate the oil with their essence; if they are dry, allow a longer time, another two weeks. This process may be hastened by heating the oil to the boiling point before pouring it over the herbs. It will then make a good marinade for meat, for some salads, or for frying.

Opal Basil

Annual, to 2 feet. Leaves 1 to 2 inches long, shiny dark purple. The flowers are purplish in spikes. If spaced four inches apart in a row, each plant will grow like a small shrub.

Prefers sun to partial shade in average, but moist garden soil. After the weather has warmed in the spring, sow seeds where the plants are to grow

The tops of rapidly growing basil are cut frequently for if the top rosette of leaves is removed, the plant sets about growing a new crown of leaves immediately. It also grows new branches. The harvested leaves are placed immediately in the vinegar until the bottle is three-quarters full. Then it receives three top cuttings of dark opal basil, for color. This will, within two days ,tint the whole gallon a beautiful grenadine pink. Opal basil produces lasting color even when it is exposed to the sun.

Salad Burnet

Hardy perennial, 1 to 2 feet, evergreen. Leaves bear a similarity to those of the wild rose and remain nearly flat on the ground until flowering time. Flowers deep, but pale crimson in a round head.

Prefers sun with well-drained, alkaline soil. Sow seeds in late fall, early spring, and summer to have tender salad greens all year. Difficult to transplant except as a small seedling.

This is one of the most decorative of herbs and also flavorful. Place harvested leaves in a neutral cooking oil and allow to steep for two weeks for use as a marinade.

Dill

Hardy annual sometimes classified as a biennial, 2 to 2 1/2 feet. The plant is upright, branching out from a single stalk with feathery leaves and numerous yellow flowers in flat, terminal umbels, followed by dill seed in midsummer. The seeds are pungent tasting and retain their potency for three years or more.

Dill prefers rich, sandy, well-drained soil in full sun. Propagate by sowing seeds in the spring. If all seed heads are not harvested, dill may self-sow.

Use the large unbels to make herb vinegar. Dill in a sea green container is like an undersea picture and is excellent in freshly-mixed salad dressing.

Basil Vinaigrette

1 cup honey
parsley, rosemary, chives, thyme, basil
4 cloves garlic, crushed
1/2 cup basil vinegar

Add the herbs to the honey until it is thick with herbs. Mix with vinegar to make a dressing of desired consistency and tang.

Preserving Ornamentals

Herbs, flowers, seed pods, berries and cones, fresh and dried, provide beautiful raw materials for holiday decorations, wreaths, table arrangements, potpourri and garlands. To make everlasting decorations, you can dry the material so as to preserve their shape and color.

The best time to pick material for decoration is late morning. By that time, the sun has dried the dew but hasn't leached out the colors or the essential oils that keep perfumes and leaves and petals looking fresh. Flower color is brightest when blossoms first open. Many flowers will continue opening after they have been cut, so make allowance for this. Berries often have to be dipped in a glycerin solution to preserve their natural color and heavy stemmed, woody plants should be bent into their desired shapes while still pliable.

Artemisia

There are many varieties of artemisia and all can be used in wreath making for different effect. Varieties include southernwood, sweet Annie and wormwood. The plants provide profuse quantities of feathery plumes for long lasting, fragrant dried material. Most have silvery foliage, but some are brownish gray or even yellow green.

Artemisias are more easily grown from cuttings and root divisions than from seed. Depending on the variety of Artemisia you have upon maturity, they can range in color from a lovely, warm brown to a creamy, almost white. Harvest them in the middle of September.

Hang bunches of stems in a dry, well-ventilated room, or drape in airy wicker baskets to give stems a gently curling shape. Artemisia makes a solid base for fragrant wreaths and provides an attractive background for small flowers. Long stems, when fresh and pliable, can be easily twisted into a crown, or you can tie or wire small bunches to a wreath frame. The tips of small branches add a lacy, delicate look to wreaths and other decorations.

Feverfew

This chrysanthemum is known in New England as Brides Button. Its bright green foliage is attractive winter and summer, and makes a good border if the tops are cut back frequently. The flowers are white with yellow centers and are a long time in bloom. The plant has an odor of daisies which is often described as a camomile fragrance.

Grown from seed or plants, feverfew will self sow and spread. Plant in autumn.

These flowers dry best when placed in a drying medium such as sand, borax, or silica gel. Spread a thin layer of medium over the bottom of a wide, shallow container. Place the flowers in the powder so that the blossoms don't touch. Gently pour the drying medium over and around the flowers until they are completely buried. Leave the containers to stand in a warm, dry room. LIft the dried flowers very carefully from the medium, and use a soft brush to clean away remaining granules.

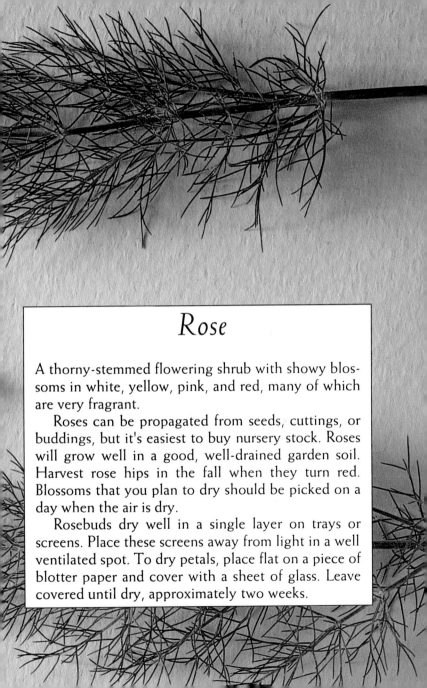

Rose

A thorny-stemmed flowering shrub with showy blossoms in white, yellow, pink, and red, many of which are very fragrant.

Roses can be propagated from seeds, cuttings, or buddings, but it's easiest to buy nursery stock. Roses will grow well in a good, well-drained garden soil. Harvest rose hips in the fall when they turn red. Blossoms that you plan to dry should be picked on a day when the air is dry.

Rosebuds dry well in a single layer on trays or screens. Place these screens away from light in a well ventilated spot. To dry petals, place flat on a piece of blotter paper and cover with a sheet of glass. Leave covered until dry, approximately two weeks.

Bride's Garland

Bride's Button
feathery ferns
ornamental grasses
florists wire

Bind together with fine wire blossoms and greens.
Knot the wire firmly around the stems, take several
turns around the length of the stems, and finish with
a knot, but do not cut the wire. Position a second
bunch over the stems of the first and continue, first
tying a knot, then wrapping the stems, this time
joining the stems of both bunches. Secure with a
knot before adding a third bunch. Proceed until the
flower rope is of desired length.